In The House

Hiwot Adilow

Winner of the 2017 Two Sylvias Press Chapbook Prize

Two Sylvias Press

Two Sylvias Press
PO Box 1524
Kingston, WA 98346
twosylviaspress@gmail.com

Cover Artist: Delaney Russell Agodon
Cover Design: Kelli Russell Agodon
Book Design: Annette Spaulding-Convy
Author Photo: Tehan Ketema
Contest Judge: Kaveh Akbar

Created with the belief that great writing is good for the world, Two Sylvias Press mixes modern technology, classic style, and literary intellect with an eco-friendly heart. We draw our inspiration from the poetic literary talent of Sylvia Plath and the editorial business sense of Sylvia Beach. We are an independent press dedicated to publishing the exceptional voices of writers.

For more information about Two Sylvias Press please visit:
www.twosylviaspress.com

First Edition. Created in the United States of America.

ISBN: 978-1-948767-01-9

Two Sylvias Press
www.twosylviaspress.com

Praise for *In the House of My Father*

It's rare to encounter a first utterance of a young poet so fully formed, so stirring and singular and urgent as Hiwot Adilow's *In the House of My Father*. In the span of eighteen poems, Hiwot addresses with grace and formal dexterity domestic and divine loves, along with the conscious and unconscious violences we often commit in their pursuit. "Everything I've done has been in Love's name," she writes, then shows us: a tongue bitten "dead raw," a girl is an "old house, burning." Language becomes a kind of haven, shelter to step into after (or during) the storm: "A hymn slithered from my throat, became a shawl."

— **Kaveh Akbar** (Contest Judge)

Acknowledgements

Much thanks to the editors and readers of the following publications, where the following poems were first accepted, many in earlier versions:

The Offing: "Seit Lij"

Wusgood.black: "Mushiraye" and "I go to prepare a place for you"

Nepantla: "Mihret"

Winter Tangerine: Love Letters to Spooks: "TIKUR"

The Blueshift Journal's Speakeasy Project: "The Night My Father Was Robbed"

Vinyl Poetry and Prose: "Father" (forthcoming)

Table of Contents

Wey Fikir (O, Love)

O, Love! He wailed. People knew,
yet no one saw when it halted...
                    ~Mahmoud Ahmed

I held a wilted fist of flowers for hours.

       Arab oils dabbed along each wrist.

August in Philly meant sweat

       in little knuckles beat against my head.

Not one person saw when it halted, it fled.

Love! Love! he said. People were frightened.

       How could they know its uses?

Love arrived, was able, could help,

       and yet not one person knew...

It costs a man his sense, his nerves,

to worry about a woman who prays—

a woman who makes God bigger than

He's got to be, she never chooses me.

Lovesong

After Ted Hughes

He loved me, I tried to love him.

I wriggled when he nibbled at my feet.
I seeped between his teeth like sugar.
I looked at his milk-tooth, rotting.
I held out open arms to break his fall.
I watched him draw blood. His drool
pooled around my swollen toes.

I had no language and no friend.
I was meant to be his wife,
his wretch. I tried to love him.
I waited. I retched.

The first child I gave him was a girl.
She fell face-first in my sick.
I fell down the stairs after a kick.
I wrung my bruises.
I brewed him tea.
He called me *witch*.
He spit. He bit.
My eye fizzed
with venom.
I tried to love him.

The second child I gave him was a son.
He dreamt, one night, I was a snake.
My husband pat his back and slit my neck.

A hymn slithered from my throat, became a shawl.
I became a liar for my health.
I said I wouldn't leave, then I left
the only things that gleamed
in that house, two clean teeth
in a dead man's mouth.

Ultrasound

Five months in and a voice comes through to say I'm boneless.
The tone is scalpel sharp, skullcapped in baby blue.

What the doctors say is only science, hungry for more probes.
I'll have a spine, intestines—what they claim will never grow.

The doctors ask to dissect my mother's womb.
In her tinish-tinish english she says *no* and keeps me floating

for four more months, building my body by her body's own
meritorious survival. The things cut from her will grow in me.

Not knowing or, knowing and wanting
to harbor knowledge between a razor blade and thumb,

Daddy says *if she's born like that I'll kill her myself.*
Daddy says when I was born his mother came back to life.

Seit Lij

Her damned daughter is a deviled mirror,
got the same face as her but smokes it out.
Girl might just be the old house, burning.

What is Love if not a maculate conception?

A flawed ideology in a haunted house.
Beyond blood? A hungry mouth.
Love spits because its desires don't
match what's being fed. Love is not
dead. Love is not a killer. My homie
says *Love saves*. My mother calls Love

God.
I know too many people with the same name.

Love is a street fight. A kicked-mouth, a switched blade.
Love is a misnomer. I introduce myself. I say *I hold a grudge*.
I adore the ballad. Contradictions still abound.
Love can't stay a myth. Love is more than who is loudest.
My Love refuses to be turned in on me like a sword.
I say *Love* so much it means nothing.
I ponder Love so often I can no longer think.

Mushiraye

I draw a wedding scene,
Emaye spies the page.
I tell her about the aisle.
Either way she catches it,
spits stop. Warns dreaming
of a knot will only tie me to
a war-torn home. I look
at the drawing & find blood
on the page, a ring around
the bride's eye. I decide
to keep my finger bare
like my legs were once,
unbristled, hinged tight.

I've grown rigid, whiskey-lipped,
gripped like a bottle's neck,
full/of violence I cannot slip
into love.

Verily, I am my father's daughter until
one day I bleed my mother's way—quick
crying *war*. My body becomes a boat
fleeing a rabid shore. My skin is spanned
& I dream the distance   safe.

I go to prepare a place for you

I can ice my own eye and fly I learned it
from my mother her late night going
under one July's drizzle through osmosis
and a shared twin bed I learned the body's
rattle after ravage after rape she left and
I was left the only lady of the house no other
neck but mine to adorn with his hands no
other back to back against the wall but me

Mihret

No offense to God, but   every thing my mother prayed I wouldn't be, I became.
Every place she prayed I wouldn't go, I went.   I walked so long I found Mercy.
      I draped her thighs over my shoulders & drank.   She's abundant
& I'm finally alive. Had I been what I was supposed to be I'd be my mother's
safehouse. I'd be her mother   land. I wouldn't wander, I would remain.
Were I from whence I ought to be from   I'd call this something else but
I belong to the country I was born in. Everything I've done has been in Love's name
& in Love's name I've done these sins: I've clenched my fist. I've run.
I've bit my tongue dead raw. Mihret covers my chest while I hum & swallow blood.
      She keeps me warm.   Doesn't ask for me to stay.

to make love

seam rip wrinkled heart from sleeve / wring
blood loose   / soak in soapy brine / use
knuckle to pull dirt up in a plume of pulp /
tempt threads close / hold heart under
cool stream / make it putter / make it speak
a name it won't spit out / pull heart taut /
swirl & whip / rinse / set heart in sun flat
to dry / place a petal in the middle / punch
to perfume & crush / add ███████████
████████ & wince at the pepper's bite

The night my father was robbed

I ran downstairs with a hammer & turned on every light.
I said, *I hate this country* & spat on the ground where I was born.
It isn't this country the Black cop said, writing down the facts
of theft. Back then, I didn't know History's names. I couldn't
drop knowledge bombs. I didn't know Osage burned
around the corner where I was bred & breastfed.
Everybody with the last name Africa was bombed
by the first Black mayor. Complex. & I didn't know Goode
or Rizzo or my own father's youth, soaked in red & wringing.
The Amharic word for terror rhymes the English "shiver."
Fear evokes movement, even if it's just a solitary tremble,
quiet shifts back & forth. I look behind me
& name Ethiopia the promised land.
I still relay its myths, nod along to dead prophecies.
I read half a halfverse about Rastas & thought,
if someone calls a country heaven it must be so.
Who first called the country I was born in paradise?
Who first referred to America as a dreamscape?
Who first felt lucky to be here galloping over all this vast blood?
I trot across the bones of people stolen & people stolen from.
Every heaven kills its citizens when they don't sing.
Alarms cross at the forearms & scream.
My mouth tears meat from bone, gleams
wet over flesh & kisses, greedy.
My lips quiet so they won't cry out.
My father asks what I have there,
in his country. His question is
an answer in itself. A wound heals off-hinge.
I pour all my money into the ocean to sit
still. Gallons of red trundle under earth & I don't move.

Addis, 2015

I meet my father's real firstborn & her daughter
sings to me. *Ha. Hu. Hey. Hih. Ho.* She calls me
akist, kisses my cheek. My niece sees my notebook,
sees I doodle when I don't know what to say.
She asks me to draw her a bride, her mushirau,
a bed that they both share. I make it up.
I give the mushirit a smile, unfurl her husband's fist.
I spare the little girl a show of blood & we both grin
about the fiction sitting in my hands.

driving without teeth

it's only when he does the rare work of smiling
that I see the top line disbanded

he's the man I've always imagined
on the way to his grave

he's got not one tusk for task
not for chewing or spitting through

waiting for the dentist to fit him with a new set
he smiles empty mouthed and shy

his dimples deep rich brown ditches
I called him old and dead before this

now I ponder his ghost hunched
cussing behind every taxi's steering wheel

according to their names

father had three children in old age
awaiting death he got one second he
soil the third he gold and died the
elders got together to discuss his
written surprised because he told
us not to talk wise man a crocodile
licking drops very green very thin
unharnessed with a free mouth went
on to a land which was barren a
green fat land for us soothsayer we
quarrel we promised not to solve
this ploughing eat the meat at the
beginning I ate all the bones you
never know when God comes never
know when we die nobody knows
how I took first if He takes my soul
run there and toil make our life's
will God's will father got no house
my father and I have the most
deprived peace the past—a world

Beneath the Lion's Gaze

After Maaza Mengiste

Each dawn, Doctor Hailu hears the young girl calling for her father, like a ghost.
Hailu makes the sign of The Cross along her battered body, places cyanide on her tongue.
This mercy costs his knuckles their sockets. His organs lose a liter of blood, each.

Hailu wakes with a long boot pressed against his mouth. His gums swell. His teeth
don't shatter, they yawn, then dive deep into his throat. He only says what he knows,
spills the insufficient truth, again and again. Every vein in his body is sore and blinking.
The Major kicks him between each rib and his body hums—

> *That's the only way some people grieve,*
> *the only way some people show Love.*

Father

I'ma always honor ya name sure you're a bad man dad that's facts from out your own mouth how I saw it pan out as a former first born with my own four eyes I sat back and wished for your end when friends said they didn't have a man who lived with them who stood and cooked in the kitchen or whipped them when they didn't do good or do enough what I wanted was for love to mean more than a kicked down bedroom door or a sore bottom those small bruisings you've forgotten are not thicker than water I will always choose the martyr over you your real first born daughter prolly loves with all her heart I love fickly yelling sickly like you taught remember when you used to walk with me on your shoulders remember when you choked—or back then when you'd fallen and thought it was something rotten caught in your plate let's face it the brain's glitch catches up to you today and I pray you stay long enough to know me as your glory I'm still your first besides The Lord you're my only

Notes

glossary of Amharic words:

akist — aunt, auntie
emaye — mommy
mihret — mercy
mushirau — groom
mushirit — bride
mushiraye — my bride, (a wedding song by Mahmoud Ahmed)
seit lij — girl child
tinish-tinish — a little bit
wey fikir — oh love, (a song by Mahmoud Ahmed)

"according to their names" is an erasure of an Ethiopian folktale "The Father's Will" from the Kaffa Region of Ethiopia

Hiwot Adilow is an Ethiopian-American poet and vocalist from Philadelphia. Her poetry appears or is forthcoming in *Nepantla, Winter Tangerine, Vinyl Poetry* and *Prose,* and elsewhere and has been anthologized in *The BreakBeats Poets Vol 2.0: Black Girl Magic* (Haymarket Books, 2018). She is a 2016 Callaloo Fellow and 2018 recipient of the Brunel International African Poetry Prize. Hiwot holds a BA in Anthropology with a certificate in African Studies from the University of Wisconsin-Madison where she was a member of the First Wave Hip Hop and Urban Arts Learning Community.

Publications by Two Sylvias Press:

The Daily Poet: Day-By-Day Prompts For Your Writing Practice
by Kelli Russell Agodon and Martha Silano (Print and eBook)

The Daily Poet Companion Journal (Print)

Fire On Her Tongue: An Anthology of Contemporary Women's Poetry
edited by Kelli Russell Agodon and Annette Spaulding-Convy (Print and eBook)

The Poet Tarot and Guidebook: A Deck Of Creative Exploration (Print)

In The House Of My Father
Winner of the 2017 Two Sylvias Press Chapbook Prize
by Hiwot Adilow (Print and eBook)

Tsigan: The Gypsy Poem (New Edition)
by Cecilia Woloch (Print and eBook)

PR For Poets
by Jeannine Hall Gailey (Print and eBook)

Appalachians Run Amok, Winner of the 2016 Two Sylvias Press Wilder Prize
by Adrian Blevins (Print and eBook)

Pass It On!
by Gloria J. McEwen Burgess (Print)

Killing Marias
by Claudia Castro Luna (Print and eBook)

The Ego and the Empiricist, Finalist 2016 Two Sylvias Press Chapbook Prize
by Derek Mong (Print and eBook)

The Authenticity Experiment
by Kate Carroll de Gutes (Print and eBook)

Mytheria, Finalist 2015 Two Sylvias Press Wilder Prize
by Molly Tenenbaum (Print and eBook)

Arab in Newsland, Winner of the 2016 Two Sylvias Press Chapbook Prize
by Lena Khalaf Tuffaha (Print and eBook)

The Blue Black Wet of Wood, Winner of the 2015 Two Sylvias Press Wilder Prize
by Carmen R. Gillespie (Print and eBook)

Fire Girl: Essays on India, America, and the In-Between
by Sayantani Dasgupta (Print and eBook)